Design Thinking
Methodology Book

ISBN: 978-605-86037-5-2

Preface

This book explains design thinking methodology that is applied by high-performing enterprises, start-ups and organizations in developing innovative

- ✓ products;
- ✓ technologies;
- ✓ services;
- ✓ business models;
- ✓ marketing ideas;
- ✓ processes;
- ✓ spaces; and
- ✓ solutions for diverse business, social, and everyday challenges.

It includes easily applicable design thinking techniques, such as

- ✓ HMW questions,
- ✓ personas,
- ✓ mind mapping,
- ✓ empathy mapping,
- ✓ affinity diagram,
- ✓ value-proposition canvas,
- ✓ storyboard,
- ✓ cause-and-effect diagram,
- ✓ brainstorming,
- ✓ brain dumps,
- ✓ reverse brainstorming,
- ✓ benchmarking,
- ✓ journey map, and
- ✓ prototyping.

A real-life case study is used to introduce design thinking methodology and techniques in a more practical way to a broad range of practitioners, including

- ✓ project managers and IT specialists,
- ✓ innovation teams,
- ✓ marketing professionals and brand managers,
- ✓ product managers,
- ✓ designers,
- ✓ consultants,
- ✓ strategic planning experts,
- ✓ entrepreneurs,
- ✓ C-level executives, and
- ✓ architects.

The book also explains how artful thinking perspectives can be applied to enhance design thinking skills, such as

- ✓ creativity,
- ✓ thinking out of the box,
- ✓ empathy,
- ✓ visual thinking,
- ✓ observation,
- ✓ asking the right questions, and
- ✓ pattern recognition.

Table of Contents

Design Thinking Methodology

The top two agenda items at every organization are being more innovative in

- creating products, technologies, services, and spaces that people love and,
- overcoming complex business, technological, and social problems with new ideas, processes, and business models.

Organizations search for a magical way to achieve these two objectives. This requires a new way of thinking in today's dynamic and complex world, which is shaped around bang (bytes, atoms, neurons, and genes).

In this age of complexity and uncertainty with many unknowns, "design thinking" and "artful thinking" have become the most distinctive ways to achieve innovation and overcome the challenges at start-ups, large enterprises, and nonprofit organizations.

Design thinking methodology has six phases:

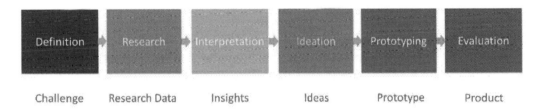

1. **Definition**

   Define the challenge of a specific group of people.

2. **Research**

   Interview and observe the target audience in its own context and identify its needs, problems and expectations associated with the defined challenge.

3. **Interpretation**

Detect patterns among research data and use them to generate actionable insights.

4. **Idea Generation**

With inspiration from the insights, generate ideas for creative solutions that may satisfy the needs and expectations and solve the problems of the target audience.

5. **Prototyping**

Turn selected solution ideas into tangible forms.

6. **Evaluation**

Test the solution alternatives by using prototypes, and refine them based on target users' feedback.

The famous artist Marcel Duchamp said, *"I don't believe in art. I believe in artists."* Similarly, companies that apply design thinking have realized that this methodology unleashes its real potential when it's applied by teams having whole-brain thinking (both left- and right-brain) skills. In design thinking projects

- the definition phase requires **concretization** skills;

- the research phase requires **observation, asking the right questions,** and **contextual thinking** skills.

- the interpretation phase requires **empathy, pattern recognition,** and **intuition** skills;

- the idea generation phase requires **creativity, thinking out of the box,** and **organic design** skills;

- the prototyping phase requires **visual thinking** and **conceptualization** skills and the ability to simplify and create allegories; and

- the evaluation phase requires **critical thinking** skills.

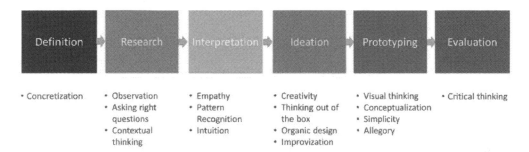

Definition	Research	Interpretation	Ideation	Prototyping	Evaluation
• Concretization	• Observation • Asking right questions • Contextual thinking	• Empathy • Pattern Recognition • Intuition	• Creativity • Thinking out of the box • Organic design • Improvization	• Visual thinking • Conceptualization • Simplicity • Allegory	• Critical thinking

Nevertheless, it is unrealistic to expect these skills from every member of the design thinking team. In recent years, a mind-set called "artful thinking" has been applied at innovative companies and leading universities such as Harvard and MIT to improve whole-brain skills by embedding art into professional, academic and personal life.

Art is the top level of intellectuality. The word "intellect" originates from the Latin "intellectus," which means "to understand." Dealing with art makes a person an intellectual with skills such as creativity, observation, empathy, and critical thinking. These skills help people better empathize with others and understand the things around them.

Artful thinking leads us to ask what if famous artists such as Picasso, Da Vinci, Dali, and Van Gogh were business and technology professionals and to look at business and personal life from different perspectives. As French novelist and critic Marcel Proust said, *"The real voyage of discovery consists not in seeking new landscapes, but in having new eyes."* Artful thinking helps us see the world with these new eyes and use this increased awareness and mindfulness in the creation of innovative business and technology solutions.

With this aim in mind, art fairs exhibiting important artworks of the twentieth and twenty-first centuries are organized in Silicon Valley in collaboration with the world's most respected galleries and art institutions.

Many of the cofounders and CEOs of the world's most innovative companies in Silicon Valley have been liberal arts graduates who integrated art with business and technology and led their companies to create innovative products. For instance, Norio Ohga, the former president and chairman of Sony Corporation and the inventor of the compact disk (CD), was a graduate of the Tokyo National University of Fine Arts and Music. Steve Jobs also took many liberal arts courses and once said, *"It is technology married with liberal arts, married with the humanities that yields the results that make our hearts sing."*

Therefore, the "magic" step that companies can take to unlock creativity, foster innovation, and develop delightful solutions that touch the hearts of people is to apply design thinking methodology and an artful thinking mind-set. By doing so, they can replace shallow, organizational mind-sets with deeper ones, resulting in improved emotional intelligence and creative empowerment.

"Being good in business
is the most fascinating
kind of art.
Making money is art
and working is art
and good business
is the best art."

Andy Warhol

Phase 1: Definition

Design thinking is not about pixels, look and feel, or visual aesthetics. It is a designer's approach that can also be applied by nondesigners to meet needs and solve people's business, social, and everyday problems.

It is about going plural and crafting any kind of challenge at an organization regardless of its size. The design solution to the challenge may be a physical object, such as a new product, technology, or space; or an intangible concept, such as a new service, process, or business model.

Design thinking teams apply design methods such as personas, empathy mapping, and prototyping. Like designers, they use diagrams and sketches instead of classical specification documents and spreadsheets.

In most organizations, design thinking projects are initiated only to develop innovative customer-facing products or services because they have a direct impact on sales, profitability, customer satisfaction, and loyalty. The return on investment (ROI) of these projects is usually very high.

However, organizations should not underestimate the value of design thinking in overcoming challenges in enterprise processes, such as human resources and supply chain management.

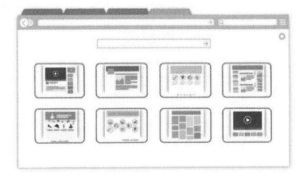

Applying design thinking to solve the problems in these processes may bring huge cost-savings with improved efficiency and productivity.

Organizations usually have three types of challenges:

1. Known / Knowns: The root cause of the problem is definitely known.

2. Known / Unknowns: Possible root causes of the problem are known.

3. Unknown / Unknowns: The team has no idea of the root causes of the problem.

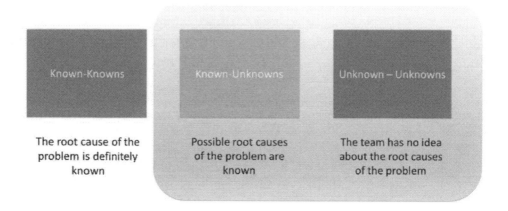

Solving type 2 (complicated) and especially type 3 (complex) challenges requires a new way of thinking with aspects of empathy, experimentation, and creativity. Embodying all of these, design thinking is much more effective than classical methodologies in solving complicated and complex challenges.

The key success factor in the definition phase is spending enough time to frame the challenge as a specific, purpose-led, achievable, and crystal-clear statement. As Albert Einstein said, *"If I had an hour to solve a problem, I would spend fifty-five minutes thinking about the problem and five minutes thinking about solutions."*

A concrete definition of the design challenge at the start of the project is very important, because all of the other efforts at later phases should be in alignment with the design challenge. According to the butterfly effect in chaos theory, a small change at one place in a complex system can result in large effects elsewhere. The formation details of a hurricane can be influenced even by the flapping of a butterfly's wings at a distinct location several weeks earlier. Similarly, an ambiguous definition of a design challenge will have an adverse rippling effect on all other design thinking activities and will result in waste. As Ansel Adams said, *"There is nothing worse than a sharp image of a fuzzy concept."*

Skills for Definition of the Challenge

- **Concretization**

Design thinking teams should have strong concretization skills in order to define even the most abstract challenge as a crystal-clear statement. They can improve their concretization skills by being involved in artful thinking activities. In the art history, the advent of photography created a paradigm shift. Artists started to produce more abstract works instead of realistic and figurative objects, because cameras could already create a perfect image of these objects.

Picasso's bull painting is a perfect example of an abstract versus a concrete perception of the same object. The efforts to concretize abstract paintings, sculptures, and installations positively affect concretization skills. Dealing with philosophy also has a similarly positive impact on concretization skills, since its main objective is also concretizing abstract concepts.

Techniques for Definition of the Challenge

- ### HMW Questions Technique

Design thinking teams can use the "how might we" (HMW) questions technique to define and frame the design challenge in a concrete way. HMW questions should not be too broad or too narrow.

Wrong Design Challenge Definitions

- "How might we be a more successful company?" (too broad)

- "How might we improve the sales of our dealers at remote locations by adding a dealer search page on the mobile app?" (too narrow)

Right Design Challenge Definition

- "How might we improve the sales of our dealers at remote locations?"

Phase 2: Research

Innovation is the most popular buzzword of our century. In the majority of organizations, the number-one priority of executives is to create innovative business and technology solutions. Governments spend billions of dollars to support organizations with incentives to stimulate innovation.

However, the ROI related to these efforts is very low. Only a small number of organizations succeed in developing innovative solutions. Most of them either create a similar version of an existing product or introduce a new product that the target audience has no interest in.

Copernicus said, *"What appear to us as motions of the sun arise not from its motion but from the motion of the earth and our sphere, with which we revolve about the sun like any other planet."*

After the acceptance of Copernicus's theory, people perceived the sun as the center of the planets in the solar system. This was a paradigm shift in the mind-set of human beings who had envisioned the earth as the center of the universe throughout history. This new way of thinking hastened developments in science.

To foster innovation, a similar paradigm shift has to occur in the mind-set of people developing business and technology solutions. The shallow product-centric mind-set has to be replaced with a more human-centric one.

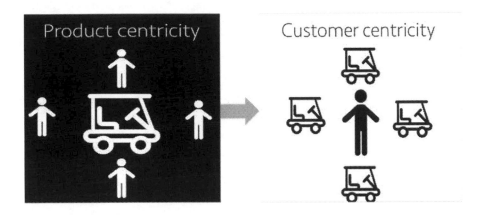

Organizations should realize that innovation cannot be achieved at the technical level. Innovation is a matter of formulating solutions that best meet user needs. Products should be regarded as tools to meet people's needs, not as final objectives. In other words, products should be developed by listening to the voices of the users.

Steve Jobs commented on this situation as follows: *"You have got to start with the customer experience and work back toward the technology—not the other way around."* He also said, *"True innovation comes from recognizing an unmet need and designing a creative way to fill it."*

In recent years, organizations have started to invest heavily in human-centric methodologies with this vision. This is a logical investment because nowadays competitors can quickly copy your company's products and services, but it takes a considerable amount of time for them to copy your human-centric approach.

Banking is one of the industries in which this situation is best witnessed. Today, almost every bank has the same portfolio of commoditized products and services. And competing with low-price commissions and interest rates is not sustainable for them. The only way to gain a competitive advantage is to be human-centric by providing the best experience in all customer-interaction channels, especially the digital ones. Previously, the digital self-service channels of banks were regarded as an "alternative" to their branches. The only mission of these digital channels was to decrease costs by providing more efficiency. With the increased penetration of broadband Internet connections and mobile devices, these alternative channels became the mainstream channels providing the maximum customer value. As a result, financial institutions had to be more customer-centric and started to redesign their ATM, web, and mobile-banking applications to improve the customer experience.

Walter Gropius, the founder of famous Bauhaus school, said, *"Building means designing life processes."* Design thinking is a human-centered methodology that helps organizations to create solutions around their users. However, "designing for every user" is not a feasible and effective strategy.

Rather than offering a one-size-fits-all approach, the solutions should address specific needs and problems of a target audience. Therefore, design thinking teams should start the research phase by defining their target user groups.

Research Techniques

- **Persona Technique**

Personas, which are representative imaginary characters, are the best way to define and visualize target user groups. Although there can be several user profiles for a product, design thinking teams should limit the number of personas to three (at most at four, in extreme cases) to prevent falling into the trap of "designing for everybody."

Persona:1

"I have a very busy life"

July

As a banker business is the center of my life. I am working very hard during the week and mostly on Saturdays.

I love shopping. But I don't want to spend my only free time on Sunday for shopping. I rather prefer to spend my time for my family.

Thus online shopping is a must have rather than a nice to have activity for me.

I usually check the new arrivals and best sellers categories of the sites. I have no time to collect and use gift coupons or discount codes. However I sometimes check seasonal and sale promotions.

Age: 29
Occupation: Business Woman
Income: > $ 100.000
Marital Status: Married
Interests: Travelling, Book Reading
Technical Profile: Comfortable with computer, smart phone user
Smart Phone User: Yes

Persona: 2

"Shopping is my hobby"

Angela

My kids leave the home at 8:00 am and come back at 15:00 pm from the school. I have enough time for my hobbies during the day.

I love watching fashion channels and visiting online apparel stores to see the most trendy clothes, bags, shoes and accessories. By checking the bestsellers on online stores it is possible to see the most popular brands and items of the season.

It is also easier to track promotions on these sites.

But some of the online stores are really hard to use. Last time I found a very nice skirt at a very good price on one of these sites but I couldn't manage to purchase it with my discount code although I tried hard.

Age: 35
Occupation: Housewife
Income: < $ 50.000
Marital Status: Married
Interests: Shopping, fashion, decoration
Technical Profile: Beginner level computer skills
Smart Phone User: No

A persona description should include a name, photo and demographic info (age, gender, education, profession, etc.) and a scenario section that best represents the mental model of the persona.

An important aspect of human-centricity is emotional design. Human beings judge things based on their left brains' logical and right brains' emotional capabilities.

And most of the time, emotion is the main criterion in their judgments. In alignment with their emotions, users first create a mental model of the products they use. This model guides them throughout their whole experience with the product. Therefore, solutions should be based on the mental models of users rather than of designers. To ensure this, persona descriptions should not only have demographic information but should also include psychological aspects such as interests, capabilities, weaknesses, and expectations of the persona. These psychological aspects can be defined in the scenario section of the persona description.

An effective way to understand users' interests, capabilities, weaknesses, and expectations is to ask their opinions about the existing products or services they already use. Their comments about the existing situation can be interpreted to understand the users' own mental models. This reminds us of a quotation of the famous philosopher Spinoza. *"If Pierre tells something about Paul, we learn more about Pierre than we learn about Paul."*

After personas are defined, design thinking teams find users who represent the personas and start the research. The quality of the research data depends on how immersive the research activities are. Therefore, design thinking teams should spend most of their time on field work instead of desk research.

They should apply ethnographic research techniques such as interviews and user observations and identify the needs, problems and expectations of the target audience.

- **Interview Technique**

The aim of interviews is to collect as much data as possible by asking specific and unbiased questions to the representative users. During interviews, the following best practices should be applied:

- Get ready for interviews by analyzing the current situation beforehand.

- Don't be afraid to ask questions when something is not clear.

- Avoid making assumptions.

- Question the rationale behind the interviewees' statements by always asking why.

- Listen more and talk less.

- Prepare simple, objective, and to-the-point questions before interviews.

- Don't ask biased questions.

- Be open-minded and prevent shallow "either/or" discussions.

- **User Observation Technique**

Design thinking teams should observe users in their own contexts to uncover the needs and problems that are not captured during interviews.

"Context" is often confused with "content," but they are completely different concepts. Context's definition in business, art, and other fields is very similar to its meaning in archaeology. For an archaeologist, *context* means the place where an artifact is found. The artifact itself (content) is not explanatory enough to make predictions about history; it should be evaluated together with the attributes of the place it is found.

Similarly, when analyzing an artwork, it is very important to know the contextual factors—such as the social, political, and ecological conditions—of the time in which the artist created her work. For instance, impressionist artists were interested in the context as much as in the content. The most famous impressionist painters were Eduard Manet, Claude Monet, Edgar Degas, Camille Pissarro, Alfred Sisley, and Pierre-August Renoir, and they predominantly painted landscapes and scenes from life and captured the momentary effect of light by painting *en plein air*, or in the open air. In order to best perceive and present contextual factors in their paintings, impressionist artists took leave of the studio and went outside in nature to paint. Monet's *Impression, Sunrise* painting gave the impressionism movement its name. Monet painted the same subject on multiple canvases at different times of the day.

In this way, he could show different views of the same content as the context changed due to the level of light during the day. At the time, impressionist paintings were highly criticized because they altered conservative and traditional standards of painting, but now they are recognized as the first modern movement in art.

Just as in archeology and art, context should be taken into account by design thinking teams because it is one of the most important factors affecting humans' behavior in their use of any product, technology, service, or space.

This situation easily can be observed at banks where there are many alternative contact points with customers. User behavior is different at each channel due to contextual factors. For example, while a live video chat technology is an effective customer-service solution for Internet banking users, it is not an effective feature for ATM users due to the negative reactions of impatient customers waiting in a queue.

Research Skills

The effectiveness of the research activities is highly dependent on the design thinking teams' observation and questioning skills. Being involved in art activities and attaining artful thinking perspectives can help design thinking teams improve these skills.

- **Observation**

Analyzing artworks, especially abstract ones, and trying to understand their content improves how we observe and understand the things around us. Art teaches us how to think with our eyes and makes us better observers. We start to see things instead of only looking at them. As Swiss-German painter Paul Klee said, *"Art does not reproduce what we see; rather, it makes us see."*

- **Asking the Right Questions**

Novelist Thomas Berger said, *"The art and science of asking questions is the source of all knowledge."*

Asking the right questions is one of the most important competencies in business. Wrong questions mislead the team, generate conflicts, waste time, and result in failure. But giving the right answers to the wrong questions is even worse than giving the wrong answers to the right questions. The manner in which one asks questions is also important. The "observer effect" in quantum mechanics states that "by the act of watching, the observer affects the observed reality." Similarly, asking questions in a biased way affects the objectivity of the answers.

As they spend more time analyzing artworks, design thinking teams start to ask more to the point questions:

- "What was the aim of the artist in making this painting?"
- "Why is this painting so valuable?"
- "What did the artist want to express?"
- "Which movement can be associated with this artwork?"
- "How are techniques such as composition and perspective applied to this work of art?"

Good questioning skills also improve critical-thinking skills, which help one to judge and evaluate situations better before assuming that they are correct.

Phase 3: Interpretation

In design thinking projects, if research is surfing, then interpretation is deep diving. The aim of the interpretation phase is to analyze research data, detect patterns among them, and generate actionable insights that form a basis for creative solution ideas.

While it is possible to cook bad food with good ingredients, it is not possible to cook good food with bad ingredients. Similarly, although it is possible to build weak solutions from powerful insights, it is not possible to generate good solutions from poor insights.

Therefore, the key success factor in design thinking projects is the ability to generate powerful insights from the research data. However, it is a challenging task to identify insights from large sets of research data.

The most practical way to overcome this difficulty is to visualize the research data. This can best be achieved by using techniques such as empathy mapping, mind-mapping, journey maps, and affinity diagrams.

Interpretation Techniques

- **Empathy Mapping Technique**

Design thinking is an empathy-driven methodology that promotes emotional design. It requires treating people not as subscribers but as human beings who form emotional bonds to the products, services, or spaces they use.

Therefore, in generating insights, design thinking teams should consider not only the needs and problems of the target audience but also the emotions. They can apply the empathy mapping technique to uncover, visualize, and better understand the target persona groups' emotional experience in the current situation by synthesizing the research data. It is a very effective tool to generate insights that are not obvious.

Empathy maps should be prepared for each persona group by applying the following steps:

- An empathy mapping sheet is hung on the whiteboard for the selected persona.

- The team analyzes research data about the persona and discusses his feelings about the current situation. The team also notes the impressions of his influencers.

- Video recordings of the research phase are very helpful at this stage.

- Team members then fill in each section of the empathy mapping sheet.

- They repeat these steps for each persona group.

- Finally, they analyze all of the notes on the empathy maps and generate actionable insights from the most prominent emotional issues.

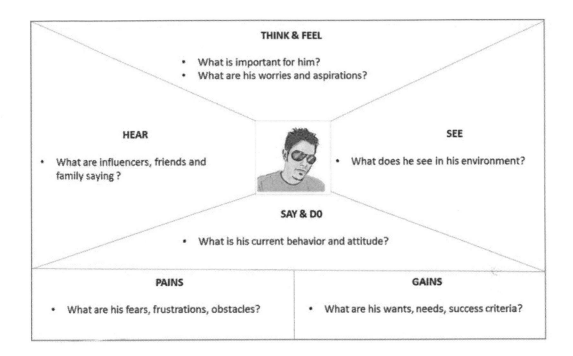

- Affinity Diagram Technique

The affinity diagram is a popular technique for grouping large amounts of research data under specific categories and then generating insights by analyzing the connections among these groupings. The affinity diagram technique is applied as follows:

- The team first writes each research finding on a separate sticky note and places them all on a white-board.

- Then sticky notes are grouped together depending on the correlation among them.

- The team assigns a category name to each group.

- Then the team starts to identify the relationships between each category and, if possible, reorganizes them under superheaders.

- The team analyzes the affinity diagram and explores patterns among the research data based on similarities, dependencies and repetitions.

- Finally, the team uses these patterns to generate actionable insights.

- **Cause and Effect Diagram Technique**

Insights are usually driven by the root causes of problems that were identified during the research phase. Design thinking teams may sometimes feel desperate when they confront tough problems. At those times, instead of giving up early, they should keep an optimistic attitude and remember the advice of Henry Ford, who said, *"There are no big problems; there are just a lot of little problems."*

Design thinking teams can apply this **functional decomposition** approach by dividing problems into smaller parts and then analyzing the root causes behind them. This approach is very similar to the style of cubist artists such as Pablo Picasso, whose challenge was painting three-dimensional objects on a two-dimensional canvas. Cubists achieved this by deconstructing objects and reforming them as multi-layered arrangements that show them from different viewpoints.

Design thinking teams can also use the **five whys technique**, which is iteratively asking questions and using the answers as the basis of the next question until they find the root causes of a particular problem.

A more visual technique that can be applied to deconstruct and analyze problems is **cause and effect diagram**.

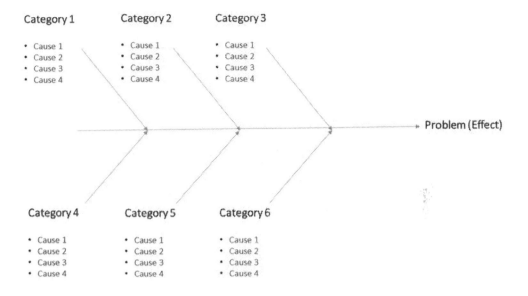

- The problem (effect) is written on the right side of the diagram.

- The main causes of the problem are listed on the left side, under different categories, in a fish bone structure.

- Detailed root causes are listed under each associated main category.

- Finally, the relationship between the problem and its possible causes are analyzed to generate insights.

- **Mind-Mapping Technique**

Mind-mapping is another popular technique to break down complex problems into smaller parts and use them to drive actionable insights.

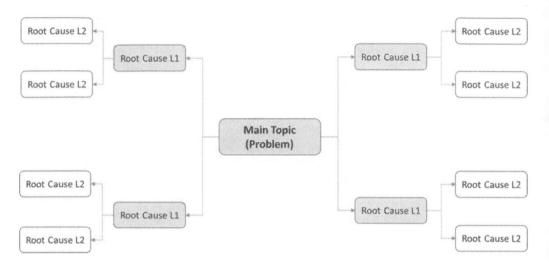

The mind mapping technique is applied as follows:

- Setup a whiteboard, markers, and sticky notes or download a mind mapping tool.

- Write the problem as a keyword at the center of the map.

- Position it as the main topic (problem).

- Separate the main topic into simpler first-level subtopics (root causes of the problem).

- Use simple visual elements to represent each first-level subtopic.

- Connect first-level subtopics to the main topic with tree branches.

- Continue to elaborate these topics into second- third- and nth-level subtopics based on more detailed cause and effect relationships.

- When the tree diagram is ready, generate insights by analyzing subtopics and their linkage to each other.

- Journey Maps Technique

Journey mapping is an effective technique to visualize and evaluate the end-to-end experience of users during their engagement with a product or service at different touch points. It provides a holistic representation of each persona group's experience, emotions, motivation, and satisfaction level at each part of the interaction. For instance, the activities of customers in the various channels of a utility services company as they search for service details, apply for subscriptions on the web page, complete the subscription at a dealer by signing a contract, get an invoice via e-mail, and make inquiries via the call center can be visualized and evaluated by using the journey mapping technique as shown below. In this way, insights on improving the customer experience in each existing interaction channel can be identified.

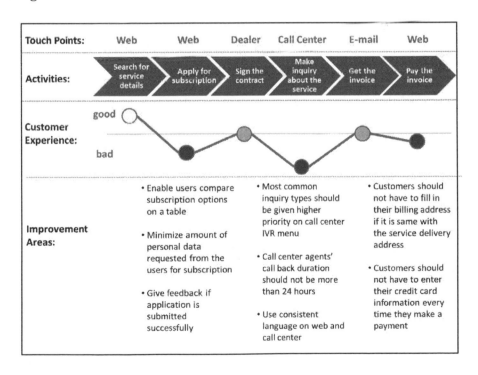

Interpretation Skills

Insights are usually not obvious. To be able to discover the nonobvious within the research data and generate insights, design thinking teams should have interpretation skills in addition to observation skills.

The legendary manager of the Manchester United Football Club, Sir Alex Ferguson, summarized this relationship between observation and interpretation as follows: *"I don't think many people fully understand the value of observing. I came to see observation as a critical part of my management skills. The ability to see things is key—or, more specifically, the ability to see things you don't expect to see."*

Harvard Business School's strategy and management guru Peter F. Drucker also emphasized this point as, *"The most important thing in communication is to hear what isn't being said."*

Famous essayist and poet Jonathan Swift said, *"Vision is the art of seeing what is invisible to others."*

Interpretation ability is a combination of empathy, pattern recognition, and intuition skills.

- **Empathy**

Empathy is the ability to understand the feelings of other people. Design thinking teams need an advanced level of empathy skills to better understand the emotions of target users and interpret their needs, problems, interests, and expectations.

From the earliest times in human history, art has been the most popular way for people to express their emotions and other people's. This fact can be better understood by reading the following quotes by some of the world's greatest artists.

The artist is a receptacle for emotions that come from all over the place: from the sky, from the earth, from a scrap of paper, from a passing shape, from a spider's web. (Pablo Picasso)

I am not interested in the relationships of color or form or anything else...I'm interested only in expressing basic human emotions, and the fact that a lot of people break down and cry when confronted with my pictures show that I communicate those basic human emotions. The people who weep before my pictures are having the same experience I had when I painted them. And if you, as you say, are moved only by their color relationships, then you miss the point! (Abstract expressionist Mark Rothko)

Impressionism is the newspaper of the soul (Henri Matisse, a leading figure in the fauvism art movement, whose objective was to create artworks that make people happy.)

Therefore, historians and sociologists use artworks as master tools to understand the thoughts, emotions, and reactions of people in response to the social and political environment of their times. As famous historian Hendrik Willem van Loon said, *"The arts are an even better barometer of what is happening in our world than the stock market or the debates in congress."*

Similarly, design thinking teams can improve their empathy skills by practicing the act of analyzing artworks and trying to understand the emotions expressed in these artworks. The best artworks to start with are expressionist and surrealist ones.

In expressionism, artworks reveal artists' expressions of their surroundings rather than their direct impressions of nature. Expressionist artists such as Vincent van Gogh, Edvard Munch, Mark Rothko, and Wassily Kandinsky depicted representations of objects in their minds instead of directly transposing the objects in their paintings.

Surrealist artists such as Joan Miró, Salvador Dali, René Magritte, and Giorgio de Chirico created paintings focused on the unconscious by leveraging the power of their imaginations and dreams. They were highly affected by Freud's theories of psychoanalysis. Their motto is best explained by American author and philosopher Henry David Thoreau, who said, *"This world is but a canvas to our imagination."* In these art movements, artists express their feelings and thoughts in a more deep and abstract form rather than in a concrete manner. Therefore, efforts to understand the artworks of expressionist and surrealist artists improve empathy skills of design thinking teams in a very effective way.

- **Pattern Recognition**

Interpretation is mostly about recognizing patterns among research data. Being involved in art activities and attaining artful thinking perspectives helps design thinking teams to recognize patterns among their observations. As mathematician and philosopher Alfred North Whitehead said, *"Art is the imposing of a pattern on experience, and our aesthetic enjoyment is recognition of the pattern."* Poet and literary critic Herbert Read echoed this idea when he said, *"Art is pattern informed by sensibility."* After dealing with art for a period, you start to associate objects around you with artworks—for instance, when you

> o   ...realize a light and shadow effect on an object, you remember Rembrandt paintings;

> o   ...think a painting is extremely realistic, you think about Caravaggio;

o   ...see a perfect combination of blue and yellow, you remember van Gogh;

o   ...view a sculpture, you start to compare it with Rodin's art pieces;

o   ...talk about a dream, you remember surrealist artists such as Salvador Dali and René Magritte;

- ...witness a perfect view, you start to think about Camille Corot and William Turner paintings;

- ...see minimalist geometrical shapes with blue, yellow, and red colors, you recognize Piet Mondrian;
- ...come across a lonely woman, you start to think about Edward Hopper paintings;
- ...see a perfect color combination, you recognize Matisse's artworks.
- ...watch a ballet, you remember Edgar Degas;
- ...are caught in the rain, you recognize Pissarro's paintings;
- ...discover a perfect use of techniques, you think about Felice Casorati;
- ...read philosophy, you remember Giorgio de Chirico;
- ...notice abstract figures on an object, you remember Wassily Kandinsky and Joan Miró.

This is an indicator that your pattern-recognition skills are getting better.

- **Intuition**

Being able to recognize patterns results in a better understanding of the deterministic cause-and-effect relationships among things.

In time, you are better able to predict what will happen in certain conditions. That is an indicator of enhancement of your intuition skills. This is described as the third and most valuable type of knowledge in Spinoza's philosophy. This skill helps design thinking teams in exploring root causes of problems, identifying insights, and generating ideas for solutions.

Phase 4: Idea Generation

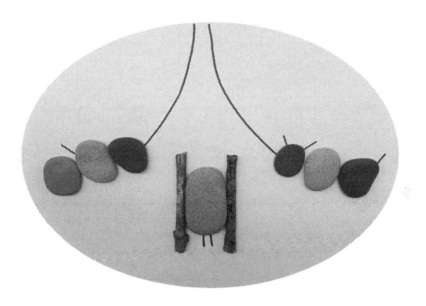

The objective of the idea generation phase is to find creative ideas that will solve the target audience's challenge. This is the phase in which the team's creativity and imagination should be at the top level. Brainstorming is the most effective technique in this phase.

Idea Generation Techniques

- **Brainstorming**

Brainstorming is listing creative ideas spontaneously without too much thinking about their quality.

To maximize the effectiveness of brainstorming sessions, design thinking teams should apply the following best practices:

- Invite all of the relevant stakeholders.

- If needed, use ice-breaking techniques (such as asking them their opinions about a popular subject) at the beginning of the session to help people start collaborating.

- At the beginning of the meeting, go over the design challenge, research results, and insights uncovered during the previous phases.

- Motivate participants to think in divergent ways and tell them to generate as many ideas as possible. Remind them that their ideas do not have to be realistic or achievable.

- When needed, steer participants to generate solution ideas related to the design challenge.

- In order not to discourage participants, do not judge the quality of their ideas.

- Make whiteboards available because some people can express their ideas better by drawing.

- Do not evaluate the feasibility of solution ideas during brainstorming sessions. These details should be handled during prioritization sessions.

- Be careful with participants who criticize others' ideas with a negative attitude. Do not allow these people to demotivate others.

- **Brain Dump**

If the participants are hesitant to share their ideas in front of other people, then design thinking teams can apply the brain dump technique.

This technique is applied as follows:

- Instead of telling their ideas, brainstorming participants individually write down their ideas on sticky notes.

- They silently write each idea on a separate sticky note.

- The facilitator reminds them to complete this process in a given period.

- When the time is up, participants present their ideas to each other.

- **Reverse Brainstorming**

If participants have difficulty generating creative ideas, design thinking teams can apply the reverse brainstorming technique. It aims to approach the problem in a reversed way.

For example, if the objective is improving customer experience at the call center, then the team questions how customers can have a worse experience. The technique is applied as follows:

- Describe the problem that needs to be solved.

- Ask participants how they can cause the problem instead of how they can solve it.

- List all possible options that cause the problem.

- Use these root causes as a basis to generate solutions for the original problem.

- **Benchmarking Technique**

Design thinking teams should focus designing not only functional and usable solutions but also desirable solutions that have an aura. Whether it is a product, service, space, or an art piece, desirability is the "gotta have it impact" that an object has on the person who confronts it.

Philosopher and cultural critic Walter Benjamin argued that desirable art pieces have an aura, an appearance of a supernatural force surrounding that piece. He said, *"A person can feel that aura while staring at a unique, original artwork. However, the aura does not exist on reproductions."* The most precious and desirable works of art are "originals" that are a result of creativity in terms of content, subject, and form. Other works of art are "reinterpretations" and "reproductions." If you simply copy a work of art, you are just making a reproduction and offer no originality; however, when you create a reinterpretation, you produce a derivative of others' work in your own original way.

Throughout history, even great artists have reinterpreted the art of others. Pablo Picasso summarized this when he said, *"Good artists copy; great artists steal."* For instance, Leonardo da Vinci's masterpiece *Mona Lisa* was reinterpreted even by famous artists such as Salvador Dali and Marcel Duchamp through their own aesthetic viewpoints and techniques.

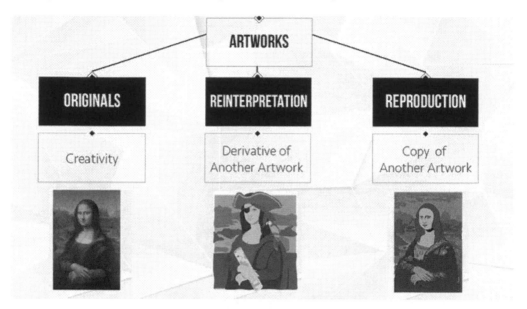

Similar to art pieces, products, services and spaces also have auras and their originality determines the level of the "gotta have it" impact on people. The most original solutions are those that satisfy people's real needs in the most creative way. Thus, design thinking teams should focus on creating original—or at least reinterpreted—solutions instead of reproducing competitors' solutions.

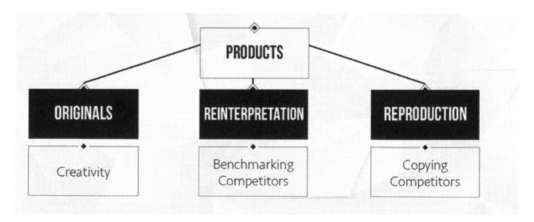

During the idea generation phase, design thinking teams should first explore original solutions that may satisfy the needs of target customers instead of benchmarking competitors. They should be like the sun but not the moon and illuminate themselves with the light of users instead of competitors.

After solution ideas are generated, the benchmarking technique can then be used to explore what kinds of solutions competitors have too. Nevertheless, it should also be noted that even the best competitors don't always do the right things. Therefore, benchmarking should not result in copying competitors' mistakes.

- **Prioritization Technique**

Every project has limited resources. It usually is not possible to convert all of the ideas into prototypes and test their effectiveness in solving the design challenge.

Therefore, following brainstorming sessions, design thinking teams should organize assessment sessions and apply convergent thinking to prioritize and select which solution ideas to prototype and test.

Solution ideas should be prioritized according to two main criteria:

- ✓ value proposition

- ✓ implementation difficulty

- **Value Proposition Canvas Technique**

Design thinking teams can use the value proposition canvas technique to assess the effectiveness of solution ideas in satisfying the needs and wants of target users. The value proposition canvas is a complementary technique to the empathy map. It shows how target users can benefit from the new solution in getting the expected gains and relieving the pains listed on empathy maps. It also briefly explains the features of the solution and describes what kind of a journey users will experience while employing it.

During prioritization, even a solution idea with a high value proposition can be disregarded if it's difficult to implement.

Value Proposition

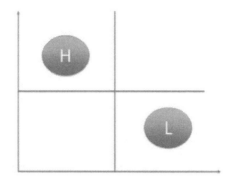

Implementation Difficulty

Implementation difficulty is usually a matter of financial and technical limitations. Throughout history, technical limitations have prevented the implementation of many creative ideas. For instance, most of the superior designs created by Leonardo da Vinci and designers at the Bauhaus school could not be implemented due to the technical constraints of their eras. Today, advances in technology allow us to realize any kind of creative idea. However, these technologies have a cost, and most of the time this fact makes financial considerations very important in evaluation of alternative solution ideas.

During prioritization sessions, the ideas with high value propositions and low implementation difficulty should be rated as high priority, whereas the ones with low value propositions and high implementation difficulty should be rated as low priority. Design thinking teams should first prototype and evaluate high priority ideas and then assess the implementation of low priority ones in an iterative manner. As Coco Chanel said, *"Luxury is a necessity that begins where necessity ends."*

Even in time-sensitive, fast-track projects, some perfectionist stakeholders might insist on expanding the solution scope with low priority ideas. When they insist on perfection, the famous phrase in Voltaire's poem "La Bégueule" should be remembered. *"Perfect is the enemy of good."* This line makes the case that in some conditions, insisting on perfection often results in no improvement at all.

Even artists cannot always achieve perfection despite their meticulous characters. Throughout history, they have struggled to create masterpieces with the highest level of detail. The most prominent example of this is the use of the golden ratio, also known as the divine proportion, which is applied to achieve balance and beauty in sculptures and paintings. The golden ratio of an object is found when the longer part divided by the smaller part is also equal to the whole length divided by the longer part. Leonardo da Vinci applied the golden ratio to define all of the proportions in *The Last Supper*, *Vitruvian Man*, and the *Mona Lisa*.

Other artists such as Michelangelo, Raphael, Rembrandt, and Georges Seurat also applied the golden ratio to reach the highest level of aesthetic perfection, as did Salvador Dali. For example, the ratio of the dimensions of Dali's painting *The Sacrament of the Last Supper* represents the golden ratio.

Due to his high self-esteem and his passion for perfection, Dali had trouble in his early career. He was even expelled from school after criticizing his teachers for not having enough talent to be able to comment on the perfection of his artworks. But later in his career, even he accepted the idea that perfection has no limits. He summarized this fact as follows, *"Have no fear of perfection—you'll never reach it."* Similarly, Johann Wolfgang von Goethe said, *"In art the best is good enough."*

Idea Generation Skills

The effectiveness of brainstorming sessions largely depends on the design thinking teams' creativity and its ability to improvise and think out of the box.

- **Improvisation**

Improvisation is the act of generating creative solutions for problems on the fly without a lot of upfront preparation. In the arts, this competency is the ability to perform spontaneously, and it is appreciated as a way to encourage creativity. Improvisation skills can best be improved by being involved in artful thinking activities, such as creative drama.

- **Thinking out of the Box**

To generate creative ideas during brainstorming sessions, design thinking teams should be able to think out of the box.

As Albert Einstein said, *"The problems that exist in the world now cannot be solved by the level of thinking that created them."* For instance, Archimedes calculated the volume and density of objects by putting them in the bathtub and measuring how much the level of water had risen. The object was displacing an amount of water equal to its own volume, and the density of the object could be calculated by dividing the mass of the object by the volume of water it displaced in the bathtub.

Similarly, ultrasonography technology, which enables us to visualize subcutaneous body structures by using sound waves, was discovered by thinking out of the box. Although sound waves are normally used in aural technology, in one instance they were used in ophthalmic technology. Like radar, this technology was inspired by bats. A bat emits sound waves and listens to the echoes returning back to it to determine how far away an object is, where it is, how big it is, and where it is moving.

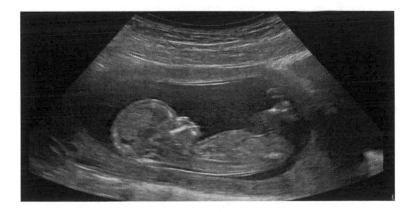

Thinking out of the box requires the ability to

- make paradigm shifts,

- prevent shallow either / or situations, and

- approach problems from different viewpoints.

These skills are best observed in artists. As Oscar Wilde said, *"No great artist ever sees things as they really are. If he did, he would cease to be an artist."* For instance, Pablo Picasso created some of the most influential artworks of the twentieth century, thanks to the new artistic perspectives he applied during his career by thinking out of the box. These new perspectives were most evident in his cubist masterpieces.

Cubism arose as an alternative art movement featuring a more abstract form compared with the conventional painting methods that had been applied since the Renaissance. It was a new and revolutionary way of representing the world in paintings. Cubism was the result of efforts to paint three-dimensional objects on a two-dimensional canvas. Cubists questioned the classical norm of painting objects from a single perspective. Instead of focusing on this fixed viewpoint, they started to paint diverse views of an object from different angles, depending on the observer's vision and movement. In this way, they could show many different elements of an object at one time. Picasso's famous painting *The Weeping Woman* is a prime example of this style.

- **Creativity**

"Every child is an artist. The problem is how to remain an artist once we grow up."
(Pablo Picasso).

Ultimately, creativity is a skill that is best attained during childhood. It has been proven that introducing liberal arts to children at an early age definitely enhances their creative capacity. However, most countries' educational systems lack this dimension. Children usually do not have a chance to integrate creativity and analytical skills unless they are as fortunate as Yahoo CEO Marissa Mayer is. Her father is an engineer, and her mother is an art teacher, so she has always recognized that *"art and engineering aren't that different."* She said, *"Engineering that isn't beautiful has its drawbacks, and art that isn't engineered is also less interesting."*

People missing this opportunity in childhood should at least be introduced to liberal arts in later stages of their lives. Design thinking teams can unlock their creative genius by spending the time to analyze and understand the work of artists such as cubist Pablo Picasso and Georges Braque; impressionists such as Claude Monet and Paul Cezanne; expressionists such as Vincent van Gogh, Edvard Munch, Mark Rothko, and Wassily Kandinsky; and surrealists such as Salvador Dali, Giorgio de Chirico, and René Magritte; who innovated creative ways to express their ideas. The creative objects, perspectives, compositions, and content of these paintings can inspire ideas for creative solution ideas.

Creativity Inspired by Nature

Starting with the ancient drawings found in caves, nature has always been the most influential factor triggering the creativity of artists. As impressionist Paul Cezanne said, *"Art is a harmony parallel with nature."*

The story of Renaissance artist Giotto di Bondone is a perfect example. When Giotto was a child living in the village of Vespigano, Italy, he drew animal figures on rocks. The Florentine painter Cimabue once visited that village. By chance, he came across Giotto's drawings of sheep on the rocks. Cimabue was very attracted to Giotto's style and convinced the boy's father to let him take Giotto to Florence as his apprentice. After working with his master for a couple of years, Giotto started to acquire the reputation as an artistic genius.

The importance of being inspired by nature holds true not only in art and architecture but also in just about every industry. Nature is in a continuous creativity process. Innovation is observing nature's creative artifacts and using them to meet specific people's specific needs. In the world of architecture, famous architect Antoni Gaudi has been the most prominent example of this. When he was a child, he suffered from poor health, which prevented him from going to school, so he spent most of his time in nature. His observations inspired his design approach, saying, *"The great book always open and which we should make an effort to read, is that of Nature."* With this philosophy, he designed buildings with "organic style," and this became an important standard in architecture.

Steve Jobs was another important figure who was inspired by nature. He revolutionized the high-tech industry by positioning people's natural behaviors at the center of the product-development process. This approach led to the innovation of the most usable consumer electronics products ever created. Jobs's objective was to create natural-born users of his products. Now, even kids can use his company's phones and touch pads with gestures similar to their natural behaviors. This new design approach made his company one of the best performers in the high-tech industry.

Phase 5: Prototyping

Even the most experienced design thinking teams can't design the optimum solution on the first trial. Good design is a result of several iterations. Iteration is a cycle of doing something, testing it, improving it, and retesting it. The most efficient method of iterative design is prototyping.

Prototyping Techniques

- Low Fidelity Prototyping

Making iterations on the final solution is a very costly approach, because for every iteration, the components of the solution have to be changed and retested, whereas changing the prototype is much easier and faster. Prototypes can be used to gather early user feedback. By prototyping, design thinking teams can be adaptive, learn early from failures in initial iterations, and use this experience for later ones. In prototyping, design thinking teams can use simple materials such as cardboards, sticky notes, paper, and pencil.

If they are creating software solutions, they can also benefit from prototyping tools that allow mocking up the solutions and simulating them by using a rich widget library.

Prototyping tools have features that allow interactive user actions such as navigating among user interfaces, selecting options by clicking on radio buttons, and getting notifications by error messages. Sometimes graphic-design tools are used by design thinking teams for low-fidelity prototyping, although these tools are not suitable for this task. Since the aim of graphic design tools is polishing user interfaces, they may mislead the team and shift its focus from conceptual design to visual details such as colors and font types. Designing visually aesthetic high-fidelity prototypes is the responsibility of visual designers rather than design thinking teams.

- **Storyboard Technique**

If the new solution to the design challenge is not a software, a product, or a space but rather a service, a business model, or a new process, then design thinking teams can use the storyboard technique to prototype the solution.

As in filmmaking, the new solution is described by visualizing user interactions as a story that is graphically represented with pictures in sequential sections and frames. It easily can be created with a pen and paper. You don't need to have advanced drawing skills. The pictures do not have to be perfect, but they should be easily understandable.

Prototyping Skills

- **Visual Thinking**

Many teams can find creative ideas, but they can't turn them into reality as a tangible solution. Design thinking teams can benefit from prototyping to visualize and turn imaginary solution ideas into tangible forms, with which they can communicate with the users to gain a better understanding of how an idea might solve the addressed challenge.

Prototyping requires "visual thinking" skills. Even Einstein said, "If I can't picture it, I can't understand it." Visual thinking is like seeing with the mind. It is the ability to think through visuals and create images to express ideas.

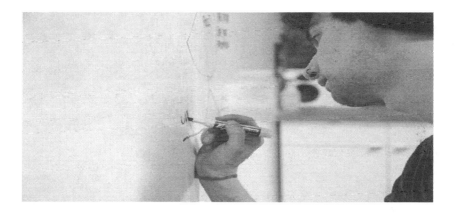

As Aristo said, *"The soul never thinks without a picture."* From the earliest times in human history, painting has been the most effective way to express thoughts and emotions by integrating mind and soul. Throughout history, Leonardo da Vinci has been the best example of this. Besides his artworks, the prototypes that he prepared for his inventions are also masterpieces. In 1994, Bill Gates paid $31 million for the Codex manuscript that included some of those prototypes. Design thinking teams can also improve their visual thinking skills by painting and spending more time with artworks.

- **Simplicity**

Even if a product is very elegant and functional, it cannot fully meet the needs of its users unless it is usable. Usability is a measure of how easy a product is for its users to apply and operate. Simplicity is the first rule of usability.

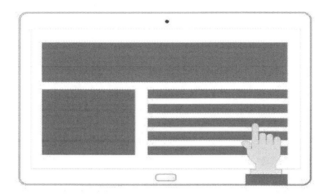

Having many features is not an indicator of high quality in product development. As Antoine de Saint Exupéry said, *"A designer knows he has achieved perfection not when there is nothing left to add, but when there is nothing left to take away."* This is even valid for artworks. Pablo Picasso once said, *"Art is the elimination of unnecessary."* However, when simplifying product designs, the following Einstein quotation should be noted in order to prevent false simplicity. *"Everything should be made as simple as possible, but not simpler."* The unnecessary parts of the product should be removed to make it simpler unless these parts clear away required functionality.

The best solutions are simplistic and intuitive ones that allow users to easily find what they are looking for and complete tasks with minimal effort and error. Complex solutions make an experience difficult for users. As psychologist Barry Schwartz says in his book *The Paradox of Choice: Why More Is Less*, choice overload creates decision-making paralysis, anxiety, and stress rather than bringing more satisfaction to customers. People fail to complete tasks when their cognitive loads reach a certain limit.

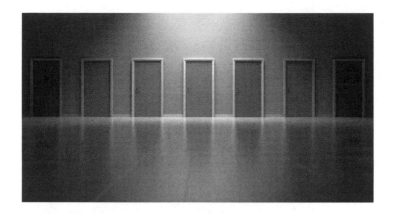

In designing solutions, design thinking teams should think as if they are decorating a small house. They should not make their users feel claustrophobic— as if they're in a small, crowded space with a lot of furniture.

Legendary soccer player Johan Cruyff once said, *"Football is simple. But nothing is more difficult than playing simple football."*

Similarly, it is not easy to create simplistic and intuitive designs. Creating simple designs requires extra time and effort. Mark Twain describes this fact very well when he said, *"I didn't have time to write a short letter, so I wrote a long one instead."* In the same context, Einstein said, *"Any fool can complicate things; it takes a genius to simplify them."*

Phase 6: Evaluation

Design thinking inherits an evolutionary and experimental approach rather than a revolutionary one. It promotes taking calculated risks by failing early and cheaply. As American scientist and author Dr. James Jay Horning said, *"Good judgment comes from experience. Experience comes from bad judgment."* In the evaluation phase, design thinking teams test their prototyped solution with users representing the target personas. Then they update the solution in an iterative manner until the solution satisfies the user needs and overcomes the challenge that is defined in the initial phase of the project. Design thinking team members should always appreciate users' critiques of the solutions. The critique is a natural part of any effort, including the design and artistic aspects. In the history, critiques even resulted in the emergence of some art movements. For instance, it is believed that

- impressionism, the name of an art movement, evolved from art critiques of Monet's paintings;

- cubism, the name of another art movement, evolved from critiques saying that those paintings were just combinations of cubes; and

- yet another movement was called fauvism when critic Louis Vauxcelles called the painters as "fauves" (wild beasts) due to the tones of colors they have used.

These artists did not give up because of critiques; instead, they used them to improve their artistic styles and perspectives.

Similarly, design thinking teams should regard the critiques of their solutions positively and constructively. They should not take personally people's negative comments about their proposed solutions. Instead, they should remember the adage, *"The customer is not always right but always has a point."*

In the evaluation phase, users have a bias toward evaluating a new solution according to its similarity to existing products with which they are familiar. When they are asked to comment on the new solution, they may say, "The old one was better. I don't know why, but it was better!" To overcome this baby-duck syndrome, the new solution should inherit the main usage patterns of the existing product that users are accustomed to. In time, people will also get used to the new solution. As Arthur Schopenhauer said, *"Every truth passes through three stages before it is recognized. In the first it is ridiculed, in the second it is opposed, in the third it is regarded as self-evident."*

During the evaluation phase, design thinking teams should get ready to deal with both yes-men and no-men. Yes-men are more dangerous than no-men are. They are silent and friendly during evaluation sessions and usually are unhelpful in communicating the flaws of the proposed solution. Although no-men are usually regarded as extreme and troublemaking users, they are more helpful in identifying the missing and problematic points of the proposed solution. If the problems are not discussed and resolved at this early stage of the project, they will later necessitate high-cost fixing efforts to fix the final product.

The prototyped solutions can be evaluated by applying interview, focus group, and user observation techniques.

Evaluation Techniques

Interview & Focus Group Techniques

Since most products are used individually, one-on-one interviews are usually more effective than focus group sessions are.

People usually affect each other's opinion during focus-group sessions, and this may undermine the evaluation results. However, it is beneficial to conduct focus group sessions after the interviews. They are especially helpful in brainstorming how to fix the flawed parts of the proposed solution.

During interviews and focus groups, some users may not provide complete, clear, and objective feedback about the solution. Some of the users won't want to criticize the solution, and they will hesitate to make negative comments. To mitigate this risk, user observations should also be conducted following interviews and focus group sessions.

- **User Observation Technique**

This technique consists of observing users while they use the prototyped solution. Evaluating a solution with a limited number of users who represent the target personas is much better than testing it with many random users. The optimum number of users that should be included in the evaluation phase is eight to ten per persona. For example, in the evaluation of a solution with two personas, twenty users will be more than enough.

Finding users who represent the target personas is one of the most challenging parts of the evaluation phase. The company's user database should be queried in an intelligent way to find users who represent the persona groups. Before inviting people, team members should interview them by phone, and, if possible, analyze their social media profiles to determine whether they really represent the personas or not. Team members' friends and family who represent the personas are also good candidates for user observation sessions. They can be easily reached and quickly invited to tests.

Sometimes design thinking teams hesitate to allocate a specific time and budget for evaluation sessions, because they think a fully equipped test laboratory is mandatory for evaluations. However, rather than being a must-have, labs are a nice-to-have facility. Observing users while they interact with the solution can be sufficient to detect and analyze most of the problems with the solution.

Design Thinking Best Practices

Multidisciplinary Teams

Design thinking is best applied by multidisciplinary teams, since it inherits perspectives and tools from diverse fields such as engineering, design, ethnography, and art.

Group creativity can be best unlocked if these multidisciplinary team members are self-motivated. Self-motivation is like a natural force such as gravity or electromagnetic fields. In order to achieve it, team members should be directed toward a crystal-clear target and given responsibilities appropriate to their competencies.

Optimistic Mindset

Design thinking teams should start every project by believing that they will resolve any kind of challenge. Despite all of the limitations they confront during the project, they should maintain this positive mind-set.

They should push the boundaries of creative expression in all circumstances and remember the saying, *"Creativity loves constraints."* They can take famous artist Paul Cezanne as an example. He overcame the challenge of creating immersive and three-dimensional paintings with a limited tool kit of paint and canvas by forming chromatic effects, changes of angle, and shifts in proportion.

Conflict Management

When team members have conflicts with each other, they should keep their positive and collaborative attitudes by remembering Nobel Prize–winner Nikolaas Tinbergen's observation that, *"there is no white or black in life; there are different tones of gray."*

When conflicts arise, they should try hard to create win-win situations. The first rule of creating win-win situations is to ask, "Why does the conflict exist?" The second rule is to find an answer to this question collaboratively by ignoring personal egos, by behaving objectively, and by being empathic.

Allegory

In communication within the team, with other project stakeholders, and with the target audience, design thinking teams should be able to express even the most complex thoughts in the simplest forms. Allegory skills can be very helpful in achieving this.

Allegory is the ability to conceptualize and express abstract and complex ideas and emotions with symbols. It is an effective way to communicate a message with a minimal number of words and to convince other people with analogies.

Design thinking teams can improve their allegory skills and express themselves in a more concise way by the practice of analyzing artworks. French artist Edgar Degas said, *"Art is not what you see but what you make others see."* Just about everyone has heard the adage *"a picture is worth a thousand words,"* but in truth, paintings tell us much *more* than a thousand words.

Conceptualization

The information age is being replaced by the conceptual age. In this new age, people who can compose excessive amounts of information as tangible concepts in a structured way will be successful.

A similar paradigm shift was experienced in the art world when Marcel Duchamp initiated conceptual art by stating that rather than the aesthetic details, the idea behind a work and the way it is conceptualized were the most important aspects of an artwork. His piece called *Fountain*, which originally was a porcelain urinal, is the best example of this. This new way of thinking had an important role in the emergence of today's more abstract and conceptual contemporary art world.

Conceptualization is an artist's composition of elements such as line, space, shape, color, tone, text, form, and depth to represent an idea or feeling. Fauvist artist Henri Matisse defined composition as, *"the art of arranging in a decorative manner the diverse elements at the painter's command to express his feelings."* Techniques such as balance, movement, unity, rhythm, contrast, and pattern are used to create a particular composition. Composition is also very important in other fields of art such as photography, sculpture, and music. For instance, Johann Sebastian Bach is regarded as one of the greatest musicians of all times thanks to the composing techniques he developed. He invented a universal form of musical grammar with a mathematical logic that helped musicians create complex musical compositions that otherwise could only have been mastered by geniuses such as Mozart and Beethoven. Even computers and amateur musicians can now compose and play music based on the form of musical grammar that Bach created.

Design thinking teams should have conceptualization skills, since this methodology is mainly about designing a solution by conceptualizing creative ideas. They can improve their conceptualization skills by analyzing how ideas are conceptualized in artworks with different forms of compositions.

Avant-Garde Mindset

Teams that have limited expertise in the subject matter can apply design thinking. Design thinking teams know that the real subject matter experts are the users who experience the needs or problems in question. Design thinking teams apply techniques such as the customer journey and empathy maps to articulate the needs of the target users.

However, innovation goes beyond understanding people's needs. It is only achieved when a creative solution that fulfills people's needs is found. Henry Ford illustrated this idea when he said, *"If I had asked people what they wanted, they would have said faster horses."* But he developed a car to fulfill the need for faster transportation instead of products that made horses faster.

When a specific need is identified even before people are aware of this need, and it is satisfied with a creative solution, this is called a disruptive innovation. Disruptive innovations can be only achieved by avant-garde people with thought processes beyond those of others. Throughout history, the most avant-garde individuals have always been artists. French-born music composer Edgard Varése observed, *"Contrary to general belief, an artist is never ahead of his time but most people are far behind theirs."*

Among all artists, Paul Cezanne is recognized as the most avant-garde, as he changed the course of modern art. Émile Zola once said that he was a genius ahead of his time. Even great artists such as Matisse and Picasso regarded Cezanne as *"the father of us all."* Cezanne once said, *"With an apple I want to astonish Paris."* Cezanne formed a new revolutionary approach by restructuring the relationship between form and color and created a new visual language that conveyed emotions to the viewer.

Analyzing the works and lives of avant-garde artists such as Cezanne helps design thinking teams look beyond the frame in an avant-garde style and improve their innovative potential.

Hard Work

Without hard work and dedication, even design thinking teams with advanced creativity skills cannot design great solutions. Hard work is the secret of success not only in business, but also in all other professions, including science and art. We can witness this by studying the lives of most creative artists and scientists. For example, Albert Einstein once said, *"It's not that I'm so smart, it's just that I stay with problems longer."*

Émile Zola also summarized this fact, saying, *"The artist is nothing without the gift, but the gift is nothing without work."* Pablo Picasso was one of the most hard-working artists of all time. He was always busy creating different kinds of artworks such as paintings, sculptures, and ceramics. It is claimed that during the more than seventy-five years of his career, he created more than ten thousand paintings.

Renaissance artists were also extreme examples of hard work, passion, and dedication. For instance, Michelangelo painted *The Creation of Adam* fresco as part of the Sistine Chapel's ceiling in four years, under extremely uncomfortable conditions. Most of the time, he worked either lying on his back or with his head tilted upward. Leonardo da Vinci also spent years analyzing the anatomy of cadavers to create masterpieces such as Mona Lisa.

Nobel Prize–winning author André Gide summarized this dedication, saying, *"Art begins with resistance—at the point where resistance is overcome. No human masterpiece has ever been created without great labor."*

How to Apply Design Thinking and Lean and Agile Methodologies Together

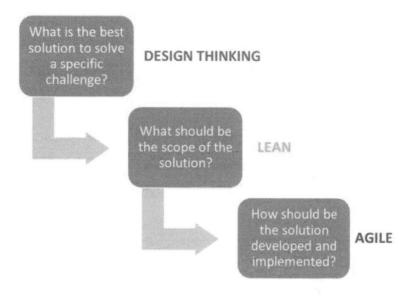

According to physics theory, everything in the universe has a bias to pass from a well-ordered state to a disordered state due to the law of entropy. This is also valid for projects. To prevent disorder and chaos, project teams should apply a methodology. Products and services can be developed with either a revolutionary or an evolutionary approach. In the revolutionary approach, the new solution is developed in a big upfront design phase and is fully implemented after it is completed. In the evolutionary approach, the solution is designed, developed, and implemented in an iterative way. While waterfall is a revolutionary methodology, design thinking and lean and agile methodologies are categorized as evolutionary ones.

Rather than an alternative, design thinking should be regarded as a complementary methodology to lean and agile. All of these methodologies can be applied together throughout the product development lifecycle as follows:

1. Design thinking methodology should be applied to identify the best solution to overcome a specific challenge.

2. Lean methodology should be applied to define the scope of the solution— especially the initial version of the solution, which is called the MVP (minimum viable product).

3. Agile methodology should be applied to develop and implement the solution in an iterative manner.

1. Identify the Best Solution with Design Thinking

Management guru Peter F. Drucker once said, *"Management is doing things right; leadership is doing the right things."* Design thinking teams need to have both leadership and management skills. However, they should always keep in mind that doing the right thing is always more important than doing it right. Therefore, organizations should first apply design thinking methodology to identify the right solution for their challenge. Then they should define the solution scope by applying lean methodology. Finally, they should develop and implement the solution with agile methodology.

2. Define the Scope of the Solution with Lean Methodology

According to Einstein's relativity theory, observations that you make about time differ from the observations of others who are moving at different speeds. Similarly, project durations are relative for different stakeholders at the same organization. Technical teams would consider six months to be a challenging time frame in which to develop a new product. But business units would consider six months to be a long duration. If they are delivered late, new product or service development projects lose their importance for the company due to rapidly changing market conditions and fierce time-to-market pressures. Especially in this kind of time-sensitive situation, where time to market is critical, product development teams should aim to generate "fair-value" outcomes in an iterative way. The team should apply a lean mind-set and move to a "good enough" solution in the shortest time instead of wasting time with complicated nice-to-have ideas. The aim should be to create a solution at the right time and with sufficient detail.

The lean approach suggests the following flow in the product-development lifecycle:

- Deploy the first release with a core version of the product, and get customer feedback as early as possible.

- At each subsequent iteration, use previous customer feedback to refine the product by adding, updating, and even dropping features.

- Iterate until the product satisfies user needs.

The core version of a product should have a minimum set of features that can solve the main problem of target users. Popular terms such as MVP (minimum viable product) and MMF (minimum marketable features) are used to define this core version of the product.

High-priority features on scope documents are the best candidates for the MVP. Medium- and low-priority features can be added to later releases based on user feedback on the core version.

The priority of features may change based on customer feedback. A feature that initially was considered low-priority may later become a high-priority one. Similarly, a product feature that was initially considered a high-priority one may become obsolete if it doesn't deliver the desired value to customers.

3. Implement the Solution with Agile Methodology

A product can be developed and implemented with either waterfall or agile methodology. In recent years, agile has been adopted as the main methodology in many organizations. According to the dialectical method in ·philosophy, "Within themselves all things contain internal dialectical contradictions that are the primary cause of motion, change, and development in the world." Similarly, the internal contradictions and drawbacks of the waterfall methodology have been the driving force behind agile adoption.

Agile has three manifesto statements:

1. "Working software over comprehensive documentation"

   In scrum, a popular agile framework, requirements are defined as short and simple user stories (as a "role," I want "goal") on the product backlog by a business unit representative (the product owner). This minimizes the level of documentation and bureaucracy witnessed in waterfall projects.

2. "Customer collaboration over contract negotiation"

   In agile projects, the product owner and the development team work at the same location, which creates a more collaborative product development environment compared with waterfall projects.

3. "Responding to change over following a plan"

   In waterfall projects, development waits for the completion of analysis and design phases. Thus, in a one-year project, it takes at least five to six months on average to get to the working parts of a product. This latency in delivery creates anxiety for business units that are impatient to see "quick" results. On the other hand, the agile team releases the working parts of the product in a series of two to three weeklong "sprints" under the coordination of a "scrum master." The team velocity is adjusted iteratively by analyzing burn-down charts of previous sprints.

Agile projects' fast delivery of working products, starting with the first iteration, brings confidence to all stakeholders and enables the gathering of early customer feedback.

At dynamic business environments in which change is not the exception but the norm, applying agile methodology is more meaningful, because waterfall has low flexibility for changes in requirements. Any possible change to the requirements has an impact on the overall analysis and design artifacts. In agile environments, a change to the requirements has no effect on the parts of the product that have not been analyzed or designed yet.

However, applying agile methodology to every kind of project may not be a correct strategy. It is still more appropriate to proceed with waterfall when

- the product has intensive integration among its components,

- the colocation of project team members is not feasible,

- it is not possible for the team members to work only on a single project at a time, and

- there is high employee turnover, which creates the risk of losing project know-how if project team members leave the company.

Organic Unity

In today's highly competitive business and technology world, what is important is the score, not how you played the game. As it was said at the start of the movie *Now You See Me,* "The closer you look, the less you see." From start to end, product development teams should focus on the big picture (solving the design challenge) by having a bird's-eye, holistic view of the project.

Throughout the project life cycle, which includes

- identifying the best solution to the challenge by applying design thinking;

- defining the scope, using the minimum viable product approach of lean; and

- implementing the defined scope within two to three weeks of sprints with agile methodology;

product development teams should ensure an organic unity in answering *Why*, *What*, and *How* questions.

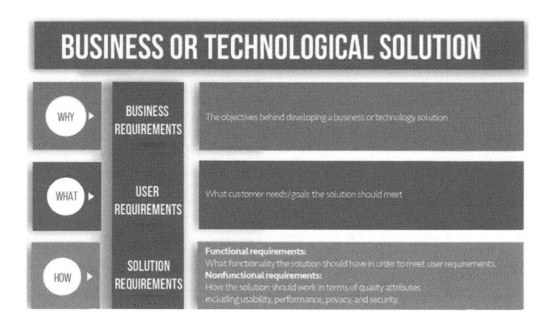

In this sense, the logic applied while creating a successful solution and a precious artwork is very similar. They both have an "organic unity" in terms of answering *Why*, *What*, and *How* questions.

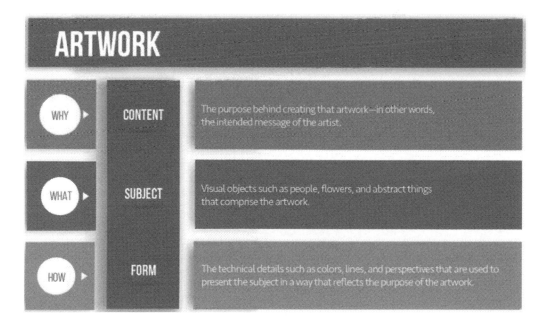

Pablo Picasso's painting *Guernica* is a perfect example of this organic unity.

Why	Content	*"My whole life as an artist has been nothing more than a continuous struggle against reaction and the death of art. In the picture I am painting—which I shall call Guernica—I am expressing my horror of the military caste which is now plundering Spain into an ocean of misery and death."* (Pablo Picasso) *Guernica* makes a powerful political statement about the tragedy of war and the suffering of innocent civilians. It was created in response to the bombing of Guernica, a village in Spain. Since it was painted in 1937, it has become an antiwar symbol. Upon seeing a photo of *Guernica*, an officer asked Picasso, "Did you do that?" Picasso responded, "No, *you* did."
What	Subject	The scene features dead bodies, terrified animals, and a woman who is grieving over the dead child in her arms. It shows that not only human beings but also animals share the horror of war.
How	Form	Broken, hard-edged, geometric shapes reminiscent of the cubist art movement are used. The monochromatic style, with black being the predominant color, brings to mind death and violence.

The practice of understanding the organic unity among content, subjects, and forms of precious artworks helps business and technology teams achieve the organic unity of why, what, and how questions while developing new products and services.

How to Implement Design Thinking Methodology

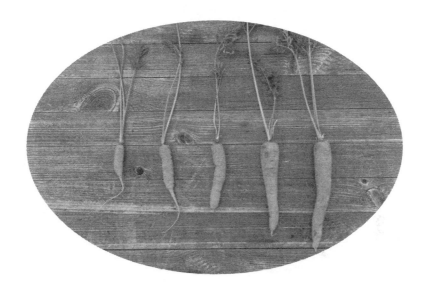

Rome Was Not Built in a Day

As Albert Einstein said, *"Insanity is doing the same things over and over again and expecting different results."* Organizations that have lost their innovative spirit should apply design thinking as a fresh perspective.

However, they should think big but start small by remembering that *"Rome was not built in a day."* They should first practice design thinking on small projects and then apply this methodology to solve more challenging problems.

The "forming, storming, norming, and performing" model of group development that Bruce Tuckman proposed is important when implementing a new methodology. Each of these four consequent phases is experienced by any organization when a new methodology is applied. When design thinking teams confront barriers raised by peers and upper management, they should not give up easily. Instead, they should do their best to get buy-in from others. When they feel demotivated, they should remember that *"it is not the strength of waves that shapes the rocks but it is their persistence."*

They should also keep in mind that *"action speaks louder than words."* Rather than repeatedly describing the benefits of design thinking, they should apply it whenever applicable and show its ROI.

Crafting Design Challenges

Design thinking is very similar to craftsmanship in the sense that applying effective techniques is a silver bullet in the design of successful solutions. Design thinking teams apply many useful techniques at each phase of the project:

- **definition:** HMW questions

- **research:** personas, interviews, user observation

- **interpretation:** mind mapping, empathy mapping, customer journeys, affinity diagrams

- **idea generation:** brainstorming, brain dumps, reverse brainstorming, value proposition canvas

- **prototyping:** low fidelity prototyping, storyboards

- **evaluation:** interviews, focus groups, user observation

Design thinking teams should be aware that techniques are only wizards—not magicians. They have limits. They can only help the teams do their work in a more convenient way.

Some critics contend that using techniques in works that include design and artistic perspectives kills creativity. This is not valid even for art.

Throughout history, developments in science not only had impacts on engineering but also on art in terms of the usage of new techniques. For instance, English physicist Isaac Newton was the first to discover that colors originate from light. He converted white light into red, orange, yellow, green, blue, and violet colors by refracting it on a prism. He invented a circular diagram that arranged primary colors and their complementary ones on opposite sides. Artists have benefited from this diagram to create effective color combinations and contrasts in their paintings.

Renaissance artists, in particular, applied advanced techniques in creating their artworks. For instance, they applied the following:

- **the perspective technique** to create the illusion of depth on a two-dimensional canvas based on how the eyes see the world
    - a **linear perspective** to show closer objects larger, and more distant objects smaller
    - a **vanishing point** to fix the position of artists to their view of the scene by implementing an imaginary horizon and vertical lines
    - an **atmospheric perspective** to show that the appearance of objects fades off into the distance

- the **foreshortening technique** to create the illusion of depth by shortening lines

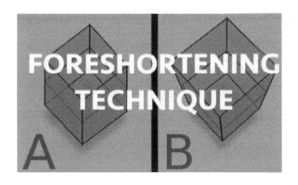

- the **sfumato technique** to create three-dimensionality by blurring or softening sharp outlines

- the **chiaroscuro technique** to create soft, lifelike figures by using a strong contrast between light and dark

- **balance and proportion techniques** to ensure proper size

With respect to techniques, Leonardo da Vinci has been regarded as the most accomplished Renaissance artist. He even studied anatomy to develop new universal techniques that he could apply to his art. By applying these innovative techniques, he created incredibly realistic figures in his paintings. The natural style that can be observed in his masterpiece *Mona Lisa* is a perfect example.

Artworks from the same movement have often shared similar techniques. The characteristics of the most famous art movements and their most famous representatives are as follows:

- **Renaissance** artists increased the emphasis on realism through the use of perspective.

- **Baroque** artists aimed to create highly dramatized themes to bring people back to religious places.

- **Rococo** painters created scenes of love, entertainment, and nature with soft colors and curvy lines.

- **Romanticism** period artists portrayed nostalgia for the past.

- **Impressionism** focused on the effects of light and visual impressions of nature at a certain time of the day. As French artist Robert Delaunay said, *"It is the birth of light in painting."*

- **Fauvism** was characterized by the use of violent colors to create emotion.

- **Expressionism** aimed to express the emotion of the artist instead of directly representing nature.

- **Cubism** aimed to show geometric forms of an object from many angles simultaneously.

- **Futurism** aimed to show the beauty of technological advances and machines.

- **Dada** was an "anti-art" movement.

- **Realism** period artists focused on painting scenes from everyday life.

- **Surrealism** focused on dreams and the subconscious, and was influenced by Freud's theories on psychology.

- **Pop art** was the art of popular culture that characterized consumers, the globalization of pop music, and youth.

Egyptian art is also considered a movement recognized mainly by the usage of techniques and rules in a strictly standard way.

Egypt was one of the most civilized societies in the ancient world. Historians have learned much about this society by analyzing its artwork. Egyptians believed in life after death. To keep their souls alive, they created wall paintings for the next life. The Egyptians adherence to conservative values led to rigid painting rules for artists. These fixed rules were called the *Canon of Proportion*, or the *Canon*. The following were some of these Canon rules:

- The sizes of figures in paintings were determined by the person's social status, instead of by perspective rules.
- Human figures all looked just about the same.

- Parts of the body were shown from different views. The head and feet were shown in profile, and the shoulders and eyes were shown frontally.
- Specific colors were used to express specific emotions. For instance, white represented power and greatness, black represented death, red represented victory and anger, blue represented life, and green represented new life.

These standards were applied over the course of hundreds of years. Some historians and sociologists believe that these conservative artistic rules negatively affected the creativity of the society as well as artistic and scientific progress in that region.

To prevent a similar fate, design thinking teams should not fall into the trap of over-standardization in applying techniques.

For instance

- they don't have to limit usage of the HMW (how might we) questions only to defining the challenge—HMW questions can also be used at brainstorming sessions;

- prototypes can be used in the research phase (in addition to the evaluation phase) to better communicate with target audience;

- interviews and user observation techniques can be used in both the research and the evaluation phases; and

- affinity diagrams can be used to not only group and analyze research data but also to organize ideas generated in brainstorming sessions.

Design thinking teams should focus on generating outcomes (solutions) rather than outputs (deliverables). The objective of the team should not be to produce fancy documents and diagrams.

Instead, they should aim to design a solution that best meets the needs of the target audience. Techniques should be used as tools to make these efforts more convenient.

Case Study

ArtBizTech
Creators Lab

1. Definition of Challenge

ArtBizTech (**www.artbiztech.org**) is a multidisciplinary group of people that helps organizations develop innovative products, technologies, services, business models, processes, and spaces. The ArtBizTech team applies design thinking methodology to solve any kind of business or social challenge.

ArtBizTech also organizes two-hour "Artful Thinking Meetups" where business and technology professionals meet with artists and discuss the perspectives employed in the creation of famous artworks.

At these meetups participants explore how these perspectives can invoke creativity and inspire innovative business and technology solutions.

However, two-hour art discussions are not enough to develop the creativity skills of business and technology people. As Pablo Picasso said, *"Every child is an artist. The problem is how to remain an artist once we grow up."* Unfortunately, as people grow up, their creativity diminishes due to the memorization-based education systems and silo-based work environments.

The only way to enhance creativity is to embed art into people's personal and business lives. But how?

As the ArtBizTech team, we decided to apply design thinking methodology to tackle this challenge.

We used the HMW questions technique and defined the challenge as follows:

"How might we reactivate creativity skills of business and technology professionals by embedding art into their daily lives?"

2. Research

We knew that we faced a complicated challenge that required a comprehensive research phase. We have conducted interviews with twenty professionals and conducted direct observations in different work environments.

Our previous observations of more than nine hundred professionals who attended our meetups were also very insightful.

We grouped the target audience into two personas:

"My friends and family call me a tech geek"

John

Age: 24
Occupation: Developer in a leading software company
Income: 3.500 USD
Marital Status: Single
Interests: Computer games, watching movies

I spend most of my time with computers. When I leave the office and come back home I turn on the computer and start to play video games.

My family appreciates my success in programming but have concerns regarding to my social life. They criticize me for not spending enough time with other people.

In the mentoring meeting, my manager told me that I had amazing technical competencies but needed to enhance my creativity and empathy skills to be able to promote in the company.

"I need to find more creative marketing ideas"

Susan

Age: 39
Occupation: Marketing Manager in a Bank
Income: 7.500 USD
Marital Status: Married and have two kids
Interests: Books, Travelling, Movies

I have a very challenging job in the sense that it requires to be creative all the time. I need to find new marketing ideas that attract new customers.

However, I have no source of inspiration that stimulates my creative genius. The ideas submitted by my department are criticized as "ordinary" and "not original" by the upper management. On the other side most of the ideas are rejected by IT department because they are not technically feasible. Our CTO accuses my team not being a follower of recent technologies.

I feel that I need to attend to social activities to foster my creativity. But when I am not working I am spending all my time with my kids. I need to find activities that I can also include my kids .

3. Interpretation

Upon completing the field work, we started to analyze a large set of research results. Empathy maps were very helpful to dive deeply into the data and identify outstanding emotional points.

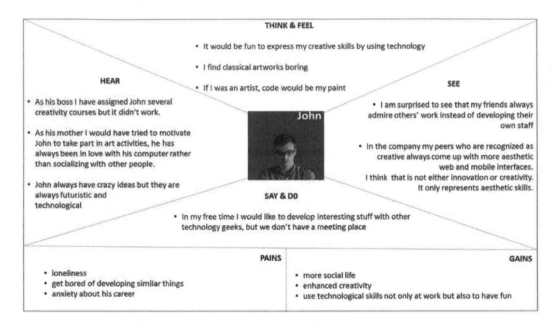

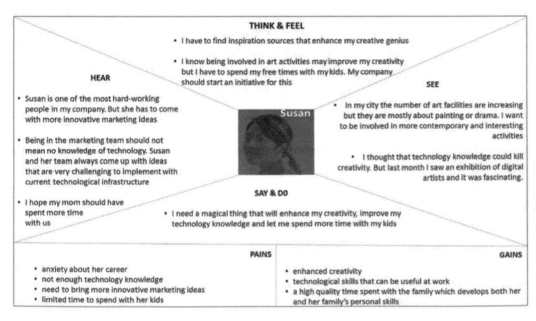

Based on the information in the empathy maps, we used affinity diagrams to identify patterns and generate insights regarding each persona group's needs, problems and expectations.

The most prominent insights were these:

- People were aware of the fact that being hardworking or talented at their profession is not sufficient for a better career. They needed to be more creative and innovative.

- A person cannot become innovative via a one-time activity. Instead, one should practice periodically by being involved in activities that stimulate creativity.

- To fully enhance their skill sets, people should not only be creators but also makers.

- Compared with classical artworks, interactive and digital artworks could be more helpful in development of both creativity and technological skills.

- The target audience has limited free time, so they want to integrate their family and close friends into their social activities.

4. Idea Generation

Based on these insights, our team organized brainstorming sessions. During these sessions, attendees were very eager to share their ideas. They generated many solution ideas, so we didn't need to employ additional techniques such as brain dumps or reverse brainstorming.

The most outstanding solution ideas were the following:

- Start a **creativity & technology course** that would be instructed by academics from art and technology departments of universities.

- Establishing a **creators lab** where business and technology professionals, designers, and artists would meet to develop interactive digital artworks that inspire innovative business and technology ideas.

- Initiate an **art & technology mentoring program** in which an artist and a technology expert would mentor business and technology professionals by conducting regular meetings.

- Organize "**hackathons**" that would bring business professionals together with a jury of technology experts and artists.

Among these ideas, **the creators lab** got the highest priority rating in terms of value proposition and implementation difficulty. It was an idea that satisfied almost all of the insights explored during the interpretation phase. For instance, people who belong to the Susan persona could even bring their kids to Creators Lab and create interactive artworks all together. In this way, not only parents but also their kids could enhance their creativity skills and technology knowledge.

The projects at the lab would not only awaken the creative genius inside people but also allow them bring their ideas to life. The lab also had the potential to foster the collective creativity of people, thanks to its multidisciplinary structure. Its atmosphere could be like that of the House of Medici. During the fourteenth century, businesspeople, scientists, and artists in Florence, Italy, came together at the Medici family home and created the most intellectual environment of the times. These individuals were the driving forces behind the development of science, art, and architecture in Florence.

5. Prototyping

After selecting Creators Lab as the idea to move forward with, the team started to design a business and operating model of the lab.

According to its conceptual model, people from diverse professions such as business, technology, design, engineering, architecture, psychology, and art would all meet to create interactive digital artworks that inspire innovative business and technology ideas.

In these projects, people would go beyond their comfort zones, and start to think out of the box. As British street artist Banksy once said, *"Art should comfort the disturbed and disturb the comfortable."*

In creating the interactive artworks, people would use technology as paint and canvas and express an artistic idea by using technology. In this way, they would remove the boundaries between art and technology.

They would be creating objects that might inspire products that satisfy various business or social needs. In other words, they would be making art not for art. They would be making art for inspiring innovative products. Therefore, at the end of every project, they would evaluate which products the artwork could inspire. Briefly, *"they would aim to find what they were not looking for at the beginning."* The approach is very similar that of Pablo Picasso, who said *"I begin with an idea, and then it becomes something else."* The artwork might not inspire a product today, but it might tomorrow. It could be like abstract mathematics. Some of the abstract formulations created during the ancient time of Thales were not useful then, but they were later used by scientists such as Johannes Kepler and Einstein in the formulation of physics and astronomy theories.

Creators Lab would act as the Bauhaus school of the digital age.

Walter Gropius, the founder of the Bauhaus school, was one of the most prominent people who proved how artistic perspectives contribute to design thinking. His goal was "to create a new guild of craftsmen without the class distinctions which raise an arrogant barrier between craftsman and artist." Bauhaus was established in Germany as an art school that combined art and craft, and it revolutionized product design. It brought creative expression to product design and used the slogan, *"Art into Industry."* It had the "vision of unification of the arts through craft." Artists such as Paul Klee and Wassily Kandinsky contributed to Bauhaus as instructors. The curriculum included workshops on painting, sculpture, cabinetmaking, textile, metalworking, and typography. The vision and working principles of the Bauhaus school have always been a role model for initiatives such as Creators Lab.

6. Evaluation

Upon arrangement of the facility and basic technological equipment such as Arduino microcontrollers, Raspberry Pi microcomputers, and various sensors (of motion, touch, heat, sound, etc.) Creators Lab was announced to business and technology professionals.

In a very short time, an enthusiastic group of people from diverse professions started to set up multidisciplinary teams and create interactive digital artworks in a collaborative manner.

One of the initial projects was "Soul of the City." This interactive artwork aimed to make viewers feel the soul of the cities all around the world with touch, visual, and audio effects. As the viewer moves the installation on a plexiglass platform that is equipped with RFID (radio-frequency identification) sensors, the Raspberry Pi micro-computer recognizes its location and associates that location with its corresponding one on the world map. Accordingly, the installation emits lights and sounds resembling that city.

When it was exhibited at a design thinking event, a group of teachers asked the Creators Lab team if they could use this artwork in their geography lectures. They said this artwork could be very helpful in teaching the location of cities to the primary-school students. When the Creators Lab team heard this question, everybody was delighted because their motto of "finding what we are not looking for" had been realized.

As a result, the Creators Lab team has started new projects with contributions from new members. Almost every member of the Creators Lab project has started to realize the benefits of being a part of this initiative. For instance

- one of the academic peers in Creators Lab was appreciated by professors when she described how the "Soul of the City" project contributed to her "interactive space design" master thesis—which was an important milestone in her academic career;

- another peer was hired by the IT department of a leading bank when he proved his creativity and technical skills with his exceptional contribution to "Einstein's Letter on the Universal Force of Love," an interactive artwork project;

- his colleague, who was responsible for interaction design and video animation in the same artwork, was accepted by one of the leading design companies on the reference of an executive peer at the Creators Lab project;

- in the "Invisible Connections of People" project, the team successfully used IOT (internet of things) technology and the technical architect of this project was invited to be an IOT instructor at a training company by a person he met at an exhibit of this artwork;

- the coordinator of Creators Lab, who had greatly contributed to the fast progress of the initiative, was accepted in a marketing and communications master program at a highly reputable university; and

- management of Creators Lab was taken over by an expert on human-robotics interaction and two experienced business professionals who had previously served in executive roles of multinational companies.

During the evaluation phase, many academics and students applied to take part in Creators Lab. The team had decided to extend the target audience to include academics and students as well as business and technology professionals. A new initiative called the Academic Creativity & Innovation Program has been started under Creators Lab. Now academics and students can also use the Creators Lab facilities and equipment of Creators Lab, which are funded by sponsorships.

We have realized many collaboration areas with other innovation oriented communities such as the "Makers." We have decided to support each other during the projects to achieve unity in "thinking, creating, designing, and making." We organized joint events and exhibitions.

Another lessons-learned during the evaluation phase was understanding of people's desire to present their work to other people. To satisfy this need, Creators Lab has started to organize exhibitions in collaboration with respected galleries and museums. The Creators Lab team also has started to apply to international arts and technology competitions and exhibitions to present their artworks to peers in other countries.

The team is now planning to expand the Creators Lab to new cities based on the lessons learned during the evaluation phase. Its objective is to help more people attain artful thinking perspectives and be more creative and successful both in their personal and business lives.

About Emrah Yayici

Emrah Yayici is an ArtBizTech (www.artbiztech.org) board member.

He is the author of the best-selling *Business Analysis Methodology Book, Business Analyst's Mentor Book, UX Design and Usability Mentor Book, and Creativity: Artful Thinking for Innovative Business and Technology.*

He is a managing partner of UXservices, BA-Works and Keytorc. He started his career as a technology and management consultant at Arthur Andersen and Accenture. Afterward, he led global enterprise-transformation projects at Beko-Grundig Electronics.

During his career, he has managed multinational and cross-functional project teams in banking, insurance, telecommunications, media, consumer electronics, IT industries, and start-ups.

Emrah Yayici contributes to IIBA® (International Institute of Business Analysis) as a chapter president. He has also contributed to UXPA (User Experience Professionals Association) as a member and to ISTQB® (International Software Testing Board) as a former international board member.

He is now sharing his experience in design thinking, business analysis, entrepreneurship, product management, product development, customer experience design, UX design, and usability by publishing articles and books, leading training sessions, and speaking at conferences.

Made in the USA
Middletown, DE
17 May 2019